Evaluating a
Student Teacher

Student Teaching: The Cooperating Teacher Series

This series is designed exclusively for cooperating teachers. We like to say, "These are the little instruction books that should have come with the student teacher!" The series acknowledges the cooperating teacher's important role in the student teaching experience and gives key guidance for effective supervision:

Book 1: *Preparing for a Student Teacher*
Book 2: *Coaching a Student Teacher*
Book 3: *Evaluating a Student Teacher*

The series is available as a set and as individual books so readers can explore the cooperating teacher role in totality or use the book that meets their current need. Each book offers essential techniques and practical advice. The user-friendly format provides a quick resource for the busy cooperating teacher to use in guiding the student teacher through a successful student teaching experience.

Evaluating a Student Teacher

Marvin A. Henry and Ann Weber

ROWMAN & LITTLEFIELD
Lanham • Boulder • New York • London

Published by Rowman & Littlefield
A wholly owned subsidiary of The Rowman & Littlefield Publishing Group, Inc.
4501 Forbes Boulevard, Suite 200, Lanham, Maryland 20706
www.rowman.com

Unit A, Whitacre Mews, 26-34 Stannary Street, London SE11 4AB

British Library Cataloguing in Publication Information Available

Library of Congress Cataloging-in-Publication Data

Names: Henry, Marvin A., author. | Weber, Ann, author.
Title: Evaluating a student teacher / Marvin A. Henry and Ann Weber.
Description: Lanham : Rowman & Littlefield, [2016] | Series: Student teaching
  : the cooperating teacher series | Includes bibliographical references.
Identifiers: LCCN 2016013823 | ISBN 9781475828160 (pbk. : alk. paper) |
  ISBN 9781475828177 (electronic)
Subjects: LCSH: Student teachers—Rating of—United States. |
  Teachers—Training of—United States—Evaluation.
Classification: LCC LB2157.U5 H47 2016 | DDC 370.71/1—dc23 LC record
available at https://lccn.loc.gov/2016013823

∞™ The paper used in this publication meets the minimum requirements of
American National Standard for Information Sciences—Permanence of Paper
for Printed Library Materials, ANSI/NISO Z39.48-1992.

Printed in the United States of America

Contents

Preface

This book is the final in our series of what we like to call, "The little books that should come with your student teacher!" In our passion for the teaching profession, we have vowed to try and do something to better prepare cooperating teachers for the what-do-I-do-now moments in their supervisory role during student teaching.

You are the experienced practitioner in whose hands a student teacher has been placed. Once the wave of excitement settles, you will realize the immense responsibility you bear for the development of your student teacher, his or her future students, and the teaching profession as a whole. Being a cooperating teacher to a student teacher requires a special set of supervisory skills. This series is designed to lay the foundation for your crucial role in shaping a future teacher.

Much of this series is generated from our full text, *Supervising Student Teachers: The Professional Way*, seventh edition. You are encouraged to explore additional concepts and practical advice by reading more deeply in the expanded version, but for now, this series is a quick way to access key points for your important cooperating teacher role.

We believe that every cooperating teacher has different needs based upon where she or he falls in the timeline of the student teaching experience. Therefore, we have designed this three-volume series to focus on the following stages of the cooperating teacher role: preparation, coaching, and evaluation. Cooperating teachers can use each book in the series as a guide for their current situation, or use each to provide a heads-up for upcoming supervisory responsibilities.

In the first book of our series, we acquainted you with ways to prepare for the arrival of the student teacher and to prepare the guiding plan for the overall student teaching experience. The second book centered on observing and conferencing with your student teacher and also supervising your student teacher's lesson plans and school-related experiences. This final book examines the evaluation process, how to write letters of recommendation, and some troublesome student teaching situations including legal aspects.

Inside this book, you will find research and experience combined and illustrated with handy to-do checklists, focused bullet points, and helpful examples. Each chapter begins with a clipped "Note to Self" for readers to jot their ideas regarding the topic. The size and setup make each book a practical and useful companion.

Note our use of certain terminology in the book. We refer to the classroom instructor at the clinic school site as a *cooperating teacher* (CT). The candidate seeking a teaching degree is referred to as the *student teacher* (ST). The person who represents the university or college in a supervisory role is referred to as the *college supervisor* (CS). The use of pronouns that refer to men and women in these roles has been met by using "he" or "she" interchangeably.

We hope you enjoy the cooperating teacher journey as much as we have enjoyed preparing the map for you!

Ann Weber & Marvin Henry

Acknowledgments

Thank you to those heralded and unheralded cooperating teachers who supervise our future teachers. Our enlightening interactions with you and our earnest study of your role have helped in the evolution of this series which is designed to guide you on the path to professional supervision of student teachers.

Chapter 1

Should I Be Aware of Any Legal Matters?

We live in a society that often turns to legal action to solve problems. Teachers and school corporations are increasingly becoming the targets of litigation. It would be foolish not to be cognizant of this fact, even in the student teaching realm.

The majority of classroom teachers are not well aware of the legal aspects regarding their profession (Schimmel and Militello, 2007). Gajda (2008) reports that many current legal topics are not even addressed in most state licensing standards. Without basic legal knowledge, teachers are at risk, and so are student teachers. Although school law has been

1

rated as important knowledge for a teacher to have, Wagner (2008) documents the slow inclusion of school law courses into preservice preparation. Cooperating teachers need to be aware of this possible void in student teachers' preparation.

Also a consideration for the cooperating teacher is court cases involving student teachers. Karanxha and Zirkel (2008) identified only twenty-eight published cases over a 105-year span where the plaintiff had been a student teacher and the defendant was a school district or institute of higher education. This research found those cases to be centered on the following themes:

- Admission and placement of student teachers
- Conditions of student teaching
- Dismissal of student teachers

Even though the number of published cases is low, you should be scrupulous about preventing and documenting any concerns in these areas. Student teachers do have legal rights; in all states, they have the same civil and constitutional guarantees as all citizens. In many states, student teachers will, by statute, also have the same legal rights as certificated teachers. However, the student teaching situation is unique in that it is primarily a curriculum responsibility, and as such is subject to different interpretations.

This chapter notes some of the legal issues and prevailing trends surrounding the student teaching experience. Unfortunately, the changing scene, especially when fifty separate states are involved, makes it impossible to be completely up to date and to include all pertinent information. *When unsure, the reader should check the latest regulations in his or her state.* The college's office of student teaching and the state's department of education should be able to provide that information.

Approach this chapter as enlightening, not frightening. A reverence for and awareness of legal issues strengthens you as a cooperating teacher, protects the student teaching experience, and safeguards your student teacher.

STUDENT TEACHER EVALUATIONS

Since this book focuses on the evaluation of the student teacher, it seems appropriate to begin our discussion with the legality of student teacher evaluation. Cooperating teachers are involved in the evaluation process of the student teacher. Case law affirms the principle that professionals have the right, obligation, authority, and ability to evaluate teacher candidates. However, the courts insist that due process be exercised. While more due process information will be shared in the next section, the following checklist will help to constitute due process in regard to the process of evaluating your student teacher:

☐ Review the evaluation instrument and its interpretation with the student teacher.
☐ Regularly observe and collect data on the student teacher.
☐ Critique and analyze the student teacher's skills and disposition.
☐ Routinely provide the student teacher with written and verbal feedback.
☐ Discuss completed evaluation forms with the student teacher.

The key to good evaluation, as well as due process, seems to be regular, open communication. When evaluation becomes an integral part of student teaching and the student teacher is informed of and participates in the process, the outcome is almost certain to be meaningful and valid.

A point worth noting is that care should be taken in regard to the privacy of your student teacher's evaluative records. The Family Education Rights Protection Act (FERPA) rights are transferred from the parents to the student at the age of eighteen or upon entering a postsecondary institution at any age. You need to be cognizant of respecting those rights and protections. Limit evaluation records and discussions to appropriate college personnel and the student teacher. Disclosure to parents, non-essential colleagues, and hiring authorities is not advised unless consent is provided. If you are not already familiar with them, you may wish to examine FERPA statutes further and discuss procedures with legal counsel.

DUE PROCESS FOR STUDENT TEACHERS

The Missouri case (*Aubuchon v. Olsen*, 1979) alerts supervisory and administrative personnel to the importance of developing specific due process procedures for student teachers while meeting constitutional demands and also protecting the integrity of student teaching programs. The following examples provide common procedures used to ensure due process for student teachers:

• Develop a written list of student teacher expectations and student teaching requirements. Many colleges have handbooks with these items clearly defined for the triad (student teachers, cooperating teachers, and college supervisors).

- Write a description of the roles and responsibilities for each member of the student teaching triad and arrange some type of training or orientation.
- Provide a clear description of the evaluation criteria, including the grading process. The evaluation should align with the originally defined expectations and requirements.
- Observe the student teacher regularly, both formally and informally. Data should be recorded, analyzed, and used for the facilitation of the student teacher's growth.
- Give timely and regular feedback to the student teacher for the intention of improvement. A written factual trail will document key topics of discussion, data collected, and specific goals for the student teacher to address. Many cooperating teachers provide a duplicate copy of goals to the student teacher and follow up with feedback on these goals as the experience progresses.
- Schedule timely, regular, and adequate conferencing times for updates on instruction, classroom activities, pupils, professionalism, supervisory input, and the student teacher's questions and concerns.
- Establish the student teaching experience as a part of the college curriculum. As such, the student teacher has obligations to his or her college and academic program, whether on campus or at the clinical site.

As a cooperating teacher, the importance of documentation cannot be stressed enough. In reviewing for due process, it is essential that you have a trail of written and dated notes about student teaching situations. Another reminder is that the college supervisor and your school administrator should also be promptly consulted and updated on potential legal or ethical situations.

LIABILITY OF STUDENT TEACHERS

You may wonder about the degree of liability that a student teacher has while performing and assisting in the role of a teacher. The extent of protections vary, but most stipulate that to be covered for liability, student teachers must be acting without malicious intent and must be acting within the scope of their assigned duties. Most states have provisions in their statutes which grant student teachers the same protection as regularly certified teachers, and many are given protection under school district policies as well.

The mere fact that student teachers are not certified does not absolve them of their responsibility for their actions with pupils. Likewise, having a student teacher does not absolve you of your responsibility to your pupils. As a cooperating teacher, your approval and awareness of what is planned by the student teacher is prudent for the safety and legal protection of your pupils, your student teacher, and yourself.

COPYRIGHT INFRINGEMENT

Student teachers are bombarded with instructional ideas from numerous media sources. Often, copyright is infringed upon when the instructor gets caught up in the excitement of planning lessons and engaging pupils. The law, however, should be followed in order to respect the intellectual property of others and to act as a model for pupils.

Part of the copyright infringement problem exists when instructors are not aware of the law. Can a teacher make copies of a workbook page for the whole class? Can a learner use graphics found anywhere online for a webpage that she is designing for a homework assignment? Can an educational program on television be recorded and used in the classroom? Does the "For Home Use Only" notation found on many videos apply if it is used in the classroom?

Student teachers should not be left in the dark about basic copyright laws. Simpson (2002) notes that legal action against schools is increasing. It is important that student teachers are aware of their copyright limits as instructors and the limits of their pupils.

SUBSTITUTE TEACHING

Frequently, questions arise regarding the legality of a student teacher acting as a substitute when a teacher is absent from the host school. Most judiciary and attorney general opinions infer that student teachers have no authority to substitute teach (Hall, 1990). Generally, student teachers are not legally allowed to serve as substitute teachers because they are not licensed and are still in a training program.

Keeping in mind the college's perspective, a student teacher has to technically be released from the student teaching experience in order to fulfill the role of a substitute. Few programs will extend their program to accommodate such interruptions. Secondly, some states have requirements and a registration process for substitute teachers, and the student teacher may not have time to meet those obligations. Third, as a substitute, the student teacher should be paid for substituting. In contrast, their peers would be teaching as part of their required program.

While asking a student teacher to substitute may initially sound like a good idea, many potentially adverse situations could arise. Along with the legal ramifications, the development of the student teacher can be hampered. The cooperating teacher may need to advocate against substituting during student teaching since the student teacher may feel overpowered by an administrative request, unaware of the potential problematic situation, or excited about the opportunity.

ETHICS IN TEACHER EDUCATION

There is often a difference between "doing things right" and "doing the right thing." In examining these two phrases, the difference between legal and ethical behavior becomes apparent. While teachers need to operate within the law at all times ("doing things right"), there are many times when ethical considerations ("doing the right thing") need to guide the behavior of educators.

Your student teacher will likely come across numerous situations that will require him or her to make judgments and difficult decisions for which they may feel ill equipped. An excellent way for the cooperating teacher to help student teachers form ethical dispositions is to model exemplary behavior in interactions with pupils, parents, and colleagues. Initiating serious discussion about professional behavior and choices may feel delicate, but addressing such issues proactively can fuel appropriate decisions.

While not every individual will come to the same conclusion about the ethical course of action when faced with a difficult decision, Freeman (2000) states that professional organizations have established codes of ethics that their members agree will be used to guide their practice. For example, both the National Education Association (NEA) and the Association of American Educators (AAE) embrace the highest standard of ethical conduct for educators. Within their principles, appropriate conduct for educators is delineated in regard to such matters as the students, school community, teaching and learning, and the profession.

TOPICS FOR DISCUSSION

Teachers and student teachers should not be expected to be experts on educational law, but they should have a working knowledge of legal issues that impact their professional actions and duties. To this end, Monts (1998) surveyed public school administrators to identify laws which they believed student teachers should be well versed in as they begin their professional experience. The following is a list of twelve critical legal topics for preservice teachers to be aware of:

☐ Child abuse
☐ Corporal punishment and discipline
☐ Due process
☐ Family Education Rights and Privacy Act
☐ First aid and medication
☐ Liability insurance
☐ Negligence
☐ Permission slips
☐ Physical contact
☐ Rights of children with disabilities
☐ Search and seizure
☐ Time spent alone with students

Eckes (2008) goes further. She analyzed school law textbooks as well as literature that extracted topic ideas from school administrators, teachers, law professors, attorneys, and court cases. This produced the following checklist of recommended topics, which can be used in discussion with your student teacher:

☐ Student issues: student expression, religion in school
☐ Employment issues: teacher dismissal, teacher expression, employment discrimination, collective bargaining
☐ Other legal issues: special education, teacher liability, harassment and abuse, student discipline, instructional issues

While every incident has its nuances, student teachers need some working knowledge of these issues as part of their career repertoire. Discussion of the above items can become part of the professional dialogue with your student teacher. Impressing the importance of these topics on your student teacher and providing guidance for teacher action will benefit him or her during the student teaching phase and throughout her career.

If you do not know the appropriate action for an educator on any of the topics in the lists above, it is urgent to seek information from a trusted administrator or other reliable sources. You can also find more in chapter 10 of *Supervising Student Teachers: The Professional Way,* seventh edition (Henry and Weber, 2010).

You hold responsibility for what happens in the classroom, even when your student teacher is conducting the class. This realization is not meant to scare you or cause you to fret over every decision, good or poor, that your student teacher makes. Your student teacher's growth is ongoing, and less-than-perfect choices are expected.

Most poor choices will deal with curriculum and will be quickly adjusted through self-reflection and through conversations with you. However, there are bigger issues that can result from inexperience, and those are the ones to proactively bring to the table in order to safeguard the student teaching experience. Plan legal and ethical topics for discussion early in and throughout the student teaching experience, be vigilant in watching for potential issues, and set yourself as a role model.

Note to Self:
- ✓ Choices & situational circumstances affect STs.
- ✓ CTs provide support & opportunity to overcome difficulties.
- ✓ CTs seek perspective & insight from the CS & principal.
- ✓ Not all problematic situations can be solved.
- ✓
- ✓

Chapter 2

What If a Big Problem Develops?

The student teaching phase is not free from problems. Most problems with your student teacher will be expected, manageable, and easily rectified. However, as a cooperating teacher, you must prepare yourself for that rare occasion when you find yourself coping with a difficult situation with your student teacher. Some problems arise within the student teaching situation, but other problems arise because of situations outside the school setting which may affect the student teacher's performance. Some problems may interrupt classroom learning, require considerable effort to solve, or lead to the decision of not recommending certification.

While some situations may be impossible to redirect in a positive way, most can be resolved if you work with your student teacher promptly and appropriately. With prompt attention, the problem has a chance to be rectified or be well on its way to a workable outcome prior to midterm or final evaluations of the student teacher.

Let's identify some significant problems that may surface and possible paths to resolution. Keep in mind that there is not a magical solution for each problem. Consideration needs to be given to the unique situation, its context, and the particular student teacher.

LACK OF APTITUDE FOR TEACHING

According to Harwood et al. (2000), the most frequent reason for student teachers to unsuccessfully complete their clinical experience or withdraw from student teaching was the revelation that they lacked the aptitude for the profession. This may be caused by a lack of knowledge about a teacher's life, unrealistic expectations of student performance, or failure to comprehend the amount of time and effort consumed by activities beyond the school day. Cooperating teachers can trigger the reaffirmation for a career in teaching by providing extra co-planning and co-teaching opportunities, a clear plan for gradual assumption, open dialogue about balancing one's life and profession, sharing personal stories about the teaching journey, and encouragement. The following two subcategories are also related.

Worry over Possible Failure

The accountability movement has an impact on the concerns of student teachers. With the expanding number of tests that must be passed and criteria that must be met, student teachers may be anxious. A student teacher may either feel inadequate or lack a valid frame of reference to evaluate performance. These feelings may lead to concerns about passing student teaching and about earning certification.

One of the best methods of coping with the problem is to make certain that some sort of success is experienced as soon as possible. If the student teacher quickly perceives that there is a good chance of success, many apprehensions should disappear. Regular conferencing and discussion of evaluation procedures can also reduce anxiety in this situation.

Feelings of Inadequacy and Insecurity

If your student teacher feels intimidated or overwhelmed, difficulties may occur in relation to self-concept and the ability to adjust to situations. These feelings may be prevented or tempered through planned activities that allow your student teacher to experience success and gain confidence. Coordinating teachers should also give serious consideration to slowing the assumption of responsibilities and engaging in more co-planning and co-teaching. The use of sincere, positive reinforcement in verbal and written formats will also help.

ECONOMIC CONCERNS

Student teaching can be more expensive for students than any other phase of their college program. Costs of transportation and housing may cause additional expense when a student teacher has to commute or move to a community away from campus. Purchasing professional clothes can be expensive. Teacher examinations mandated by states are another expense. Even incidental expenses, like the price of lunch, lesson materials, or cost of afterschool events, may be regarded as significant by student teachers.

Your effort to be aware of and refrain from requests that might cause financial complications for your student teacher will be appreciated. You can also offer money-saving ideas and share school resources.

On the other hand, a cooperating teacher should not allow a student teacher's preoccupation with financial concerns to affect his performance while teaching. If financial matters seem to become excuses for not meeting obligations, then a conversation with the college supervisor may be necessary.

FAMILY AND PEER ISSUES

Conflicts with family, spouses, significant others, and roommates have a wide range of possibilities. Some student teachers may simply be adjusting to being away from home, while others may be experiencing marital complications. Single parents may have child care and custody issues, while others may have a role as caregiver to an ailing loved one. Problems of this nature may manifest in the professional behavior of a student teacher in a lack of preparation and effectiveness, irritation, too much time spent divulging the problem, or even depression.

When it is apparent that these difficult problems are affecting your student teacher's performance, they must be addressed. It is helpful to assure the student teacher that some veteran teachers also face these same problems. Balancing time for personal and professional lives is crucial, as is the need to temper the desire to talk about their situation to every available ear. It is important that you establish empathy with your student teacher, discuss plans to meet student teaching obligations, and possibly refer him or her to someone who can provide further emotional support and directives.

IMMATURITY

The student teacher should possess the ability to relate to pupils and teachers in an adult manner. An immature person fails to display appropriate behavior. In most cases, immaturity is apparent when the person tries to gain acceptance by resorting to behavior that is acceptable to a younger group, most likely that of her peers or even the pupils she teaches.

The immature student teacher can change. A single activity or encounter can bring about the realization that a change is needed, or a frank talk with you and the college supervisor may achieve results. Here are to-dos which may help your student teacher abandon immature behavior:

- ☐ Put the student teacher in situations where she can be accepted as an adult by pupils and faculty.
- ☐ Monitor the student teacher's association with pupils.
- ☐ Stay close to the student teacher in situations where immature actions are likely to surface.
- ☐ Provide concrete examples of vocabulary usage, dress, and actions that show lack of maturity, authority, or professionalism.
- ☐ Insist that the student teacher's work be of professional quality.
- ☐ Encourage association with mature teachers.
- ☐ Reinforce mature behaviors when they occur.

STRESS

Stress is likely to be experienced by student teachers, and it originates from a number of sources. Not all symptoms of stress are highly visible, but the cooperating teacher should be alert to the possibility. Murray-Harvey et al. (2000) found that student teachers report that a positive relationship with their cooperating teachers is the most significant factor in helping them deal with stress during their clinical experience.

Clement (1999) notes that student teachers are likely to reduce stress through exercise, prayer, and sleep. Morris and Morris (1980) make a number of other suggestions which you may want to use as a checklist for taking action to reduce your student teacher's stress:

☐ Establish and maintain open communication between the student teacher, cooperating teacher, and college supervisor.

☐ Encourage student teachers to schedule some time each day for themselves.

☐ Provide opportunities for student teachers to share their experiences.

☐ Encourage student teachers to get sufficient amounts of exercise, rest, and sleep.

☐ Encourage, or even require, that student teachers prepare unit and lesson plans well in advance.

☐ Encourage student teachers to engage in regular, in-depth self-evaluation.

☐ Provide a comprehensive orientation program to student teaching.

SCHOOL ADJUSTMENT

Your student teacher's transition from a college to a K–12 school setting may not be as smooth as one would assume, despite an increasing number of clinical experiences prior to student teaching. These problems may peak quickly, and a cooperating teacher should be alert for symptoms. Let's explore the student teacher's adjustment to the school setting, status, and appearance.

Setting

Your student teacher may have trouble finding comfort in his assigned school and feel he or she does not belong. This feeling can be due to a number of things:

- Lack of familiarity with the school's cultural environment
- Lack of acquaintance with faculty
- Lack of knowledge of school procedures
- Lack of knowledge about learners

If any of these things are a conscious or unconscious concern, your student teacher may show symptoms of confusion, stress, or disappointment. Cooperating teachers need to be sensitive to any feelings of not belonging or confusion with prevailing practices. To proactively sidestep this issue, give full consideration to the acclimation of your student teacher. Ideas and details are provided in the first book of the series (*Preparing for a Student Teacher*). If these feelings continue to exist, try reviewing the information since your student teacher may have felt overwhelmed or could not absorb everything when listening the first time. Written information is often helpful as a resource for your student teacher.

Status

Your school environment takes a college student away from interactions with peers and places him in an adult-student interaction. Your student teacher may feel awkward about taking the adult role. Sometimes the age difference is greater between you and your student teacher than it is between the student teacher and the pupils in the class, especially in the secondary setting. The learners often view the student teacher as more fashionable and approachable. A student teacher may be flattered by the attention given by a flirting student or a student purposefully displaying some type of annoying behavior to attract attention. Young professionals may not be aware of the obvious, so you must intervene whenever such problems start to surface. The following checklist provides you with tips to consider when this arises:

- ☐ Explain to your student teacher why certain pupils are acting as they are.
- ☐ See that the problem is discussed before it gets out of hand.
- ☐ Alert your student teacher to sensitive situations.
- ☐ Make suggestions about how to appear more mature in the eyes of the students.
- ☐ Make your presence known in social situations.
- ☐ Talk to the pupils involved about their inappropriate behavior, if necessary.
- ☐ Include your student teacher in faculty settings.

Appearance

The difference between the accepted patterns of dress in public schools and the prevailing pattern on campus may create a breach that is difficult to reconcile. Problems are likely to focus on casual dress and the difficulty that it may present in being accepted by faculty, students, and administration. For a student teacher, it is sometimes necessary to dress more formally than teachers in order to gain the same degree of adult distinction and acceptance from students that teachers enjoy.

The criteria for judgment should be whether the student teacher's appearance affects professional relationships with learners. When appearance must be discussed, the following guidelines may be helpful:

- The student teacher usually prefers to have the cooperating teacher discuss the subject with him.

- An early explanation of school dress policy avoids an inadvertent violation of the rules or unwritten expectations.
- The reasons for standards of appearance should be explained.
- A critique of style should connect to the effect on students, instruction, or professional image.

Physical appearance and dress for the classroom are somewhat analogous to wearing a uniform; they are symbols indicating that the person who wears it has certain skills, responsibilities, and authority. Your student teacher may not have considered this possibility, so do not be surprised if attention to the perceptions of attire needs to be detailed. If she becomes aware that appearance can help to achieve acceptance as a professional, more informal or unacceptable patterns of appearance may be voluntarily abandoned.

Also note that student teachers will be transitioning their wardrobe to include professionally appropriate clothing and jewelry. If available in your community, it can be helpful if the student teacher is aware of how resale and consignment shops can assist in finding inexpensive yet practical clothing for the teaching role.

EXTENDED SCHEDULE

Many of the problems affecting student teachers have their roots in activities that consume time outside the student teaching school day. Those commitments may eventually result in poor student teaching performance. You may notice inadequate preparation, reluctance to go beyond the minimum, fatigue, and limited after-school involvement. Here are three situations dealing with extended schedules that may overpower your student teacher's effectiveness and growth during student teaching.

Coursework

Occasionally, a student teacher will concurrently take coursework while student teaching. The demands of a college course can consume hours of time, and the responsibilities of student teaching may become less important when needing to meet course requirement deadlines.

A student teacher who is involved in a daylong program of teaching should be discouraged from enrolling in formal coursework. Although the cooperating teacher may not be in a position to determine whether coursework is taken, you should point out the consequences in the event that the student teacher's performance is not meeting expected standards. Share ideas of how to balance studies with teaching responsibilities.

Employment

Financial problems are real to a great number of college students. Some may completely finance their education through employment, while others seek jobs in order to live more comfortably. Student teachers who have been able to work while successfully managing prior college requirements may incorrectly anticipate that the same can be done with student teaching.

Student teaching becomes a full-time job. If one is also employed, conflicting time demands can create problems. You must protect your class, and thus point out the possible consequence of poor performance if your student teacher fails to devote more effort to student teaching. It is worthwhile to explore courses of action that will reconcile his need to work with the intense demands of a student teaching schedule. This may include reduced work hours, only weekend hours, a job change, or some type of financial assistance. College supervisors may know of other workable options.

College Activities

If a student teacher is assigned to a school close to the college campus, there may be a temptation to continue with normal extracurricular activities. Such participation competes for time, and a student teacher who occupies an established position at college may be reluctant to surrender that role. Make your student teacher aware of the perception and the effect of extracurricular choices on his student teaching responsibilities. Discuss ways to reduce involvement during this time period. In extreme situations, directive behaviors from the cooperating teacher and college supervisor may be needed.

In the competitive job market, a student teacher has too much at stake to risk a low evaluation due to an extended schedule. When you feel that outside activities are threatening your student teacher's success or learner progress, provide concrete examples that demonstrate weak performance in teaching and non-teaching responsibilities. Additionally, include these items in a discussion with your student teacher:

- ☐ Your reputation as a future teacher is being defined during student teaching.
- ☐ Not being thoroughly prepared is unfair to pupils.
- ☐ Your competing demands are only temporary, while the results of student teaching are more permanent.
- ☐ Your requirements for student teaching must be met to be certified and complete your college program.

INSTRUCTIONAL PROBLEMS

Ranging from cognition to technique, the following problems for student teachers seem to be the most common ones experienced in the instructional domain.

Student Motivation

Student teachers want to combat apathy, incomplete assignments, negative attitudes, excessive absences, and other symptoms of a lack of motivation. They want to secure the attention of pupils and to arouse interest in their studies. It is possible that a student teacher's zealousness is underappreciated by learners. Difficulties may arise when your student teacher threatens students with poor grades and fewer privileges, and it is important to recall that some learners become unmotivated when they are underchallenged.

Linking lessons to the learners' real-life experiences, crafting objectives to youths' interests, and engaging students in active learning are all effective strategies to improve student motivation. Discussions with your student teacher should examine their projected interest, the preparation and delivery style of their lesson, variance of instructional activities, and their knowledge of their students.

Adapting Subject Matter to Learner Level

Student teachers often experience difficulty in adapting subject matter to the needs and interests of their learners. In addressing this problem, you can assist the student teacher in understanding that the subject matter must appear relevant and be appropriate for all learners. This involves an analysis of what has been taught, what should be taught, and what the priority of this new content should be. The teacher's manual, learning standards, and websites with lesson plan ideas can assist your student teacher in making age-appropriate subject matter decisions.

Classroom Management and Discipline

Whitfield (1995) found that management was one of four major causes of concern for student teachers. Even when student teachers have had previous discussions about discipline in course work, it is not until they are physically in a classroom for extended periods of time that the issues of classroom management and discipline become real. It is then that anxiety sets in, and they begin looking for answers to specific problems (Reed, 1989).

Student teachers need assistance in establishing and maintaining an effective learning environment. Cooperating teachers can offer practical tips for coping with discipline problems, but they will have to go further if they are to have a significant impact on the future management skills of their student teachers. Sharing various strategies and philosophies of classroom management makes it a topic of discussion throughout the whole student teaching experience. Modeling and incorporating your student teacher into the established management system is as important as allowing them to initiate and implement other methods.

Interestingly, a study by Kher et al. (2000) found that student teachers lack any notion of how to prevent problems from surfacing in the first place, or how to encourage pupils to cooperate with the teacher. Proactive management and fair, consistent discipline are very important discussions and modeling points.

A good way to support your student teacher is to identify both her weaker areas of management and various solutions. Remember to inquire about your student teacher's knowledge base since he or she is apt to forget about activating strategies learned on campus. The following lists may help you determine in which areas your student teacher requires the most attention.

Doebler and Roberson (1987) report a number of problems associated with classroom management and discipline. Are any of these a problem area for your student teacher?

- ☐ Class monitoring
- ☐ Maintaining on-task behavior
- ☐ Organizational skills
- ☐ Interacting with students
- ☐ Management of groups
- ☐ Transition
- ☐ Time management

During a three-year period, Reed (1989) investigated and listed categories of management concerns for student teachers. Which topics of discussion would be worthwhile to help your student teacher develop in both technique and awareness?

- ☐ Excessive talking
- ☐ Uncooperative behavior
- ☐ Not doing work
- ☐ Insolent or rude behavior
- ☐ Breaking rules
- ☐ Aggressive behavior

☐ Inattentiveness
☐ Not staying in one's seat
☐ Being unprepared
☐ Using abusive language
☐ Stealing
☐ Sexual harassment
☐ Being the "class clown"
☐ Racial harassment

After some reflection on your discussion(s), your student teacher can determine a course of action. Document any changes, which are sometimes slow in evolving. She will need your continuing support, patience, and insight. In some extreme situations, a return to co-teaching for a block of time can be rejuvenating, since management can be shared and modeled.

Lack of Basic Teaching Skills

Most candidates for a teaching certificate demonstrate that they possess the minimum competencies to be a successful teacher, but occasionally there is serious doubt about someone's teaching ability. Any of the following traits could be indicators of inadequacy:

• Timidity
• Insecurity
• Immaturity
• Lack of organizational skills
• Ineffective planning
• Failure to consistently meet responsibilities
• Weak interpersonal skills
• Poor communication skills
• Inability to manage a classroom independently
• Lack of measurable progress from students
• Problems with expressing thoughts
• Lack of basic teaching techniques
• Inadequate content knowledge
• Lack of interest in teaching
• Lack of ability to demonstrate reflective thinking

Many of these weaknesses can be improved through recognition and concentrated effort. The problem must be identified early so the student teacher becomes aware and a corrective plan may be devised. Each problem needs an individual diagnosis and a specific plan of action. Collect data as evidence of change, slow assumptions of new responsibilities, increase co-planning, demonstrate, and encourage.

No matter the problem, big or small, rare or reoccurring, it is wise to document the situation. A written record provides objectivity and verification. The greatest oversights on the part of a cooperating teacher may be a failure to keep complete records, a reluctance to notify the college supervisor when it becomes apparent that the student teacher is having a significant problem, and a failure to identify the problem early enough to permit any kind of remedial procedures.

PROBLEMS BEYOND STUDENT TEACHER CONTROL

Recognize that serious problems can arise that are not in the control of your student teacher. If left unaddressed, these often-sensitive situations can escalate to the point of making the student teacher personally uncomfortable, and the student teaching situation may not be conducive for professional development. Examples of these situations can arise from teacher placement in too conservative or too liberal an environment, gender or cultural issues, or insurmountable professional or personal conflicts.

Unfortunately, a new placement is often the solution when an outside force gravely overshadows the present student teaching placement. Careful consideration should be given to an appropriate plan of action for the situation, the factors involved, and the effects on all parties. Because of the sensitive nature and the possible legal ramifications of the situation, it is wise for you to discuss the situation with the college supervisor and school principal and make a decision together.

If it is decided that the best action is for the student teacher to move to a friendlier or better-suited student teaching environment, your student teacher will need both your help in understanding the unlikelihood of changing the present situation and your assurance that the problem is not her fault. Your attention to assisting your student teacher in a smooth transition to the new placement is both critical and compassionate.

If the student teacher remains in the situation, the cooperating teacher must be an advocate for the student teacher each and every day. He will have to reassure the student teacher of his support and confront the source of the problem when necessary.

PROBLEM ANALYSIS MODEL

When you recognize that your student teacher is faced with a significant problem, it is important that you promptly and properly identify it and seek a resolution. The following model is a step-by-step procedure for looking at a problem and working toward a solution:

Step 1: Get the Facts

- What has happened?
- Why did the problem occur?
- What principles or issues are involved?
- How does this affect the learners, school community, and student teacher?
- Can the college supervisor or principal add any information?

Step 2: List and Evaluate Alternative Courses of Action

- How will each alternative affect the participants involved?
- Are the alternatives feasible?
- What will most likely prevent the situation from occurring again?
- Can the college supervisor or principal provide any alternative ideas?

Step 3: Take a Course of Action that Seems Most Defensible

- Why is it a better alternative?
- How will it benefit the student teacher and the students?
- Is it likely to prevent a problem from occurring in the future?
- Is this supported by the college supervisor and principal?

PROBLEM-SOLVING CLIMATE

The style and behavior of a cooperating teacher contribute to successful remedial procedures of student teaching problems. When a good working relationship has been established, it becomes the trusted, solid foundation upon which to address significant problems. Examples of actions that build an effective climate for addressing extreme student teaching problems are:

- Know the facts before action is taken.
- Identify the commitment and abstraction levels of your student teacher in order to approach the problem with an effective conferencing strategy. (See the second book in this series, *Coaching a Student Teacher.*)
- Put problems in context.
- Discuss the problem with your student teacher in an objective manner by using concrete examples and data.
- Express confidence in your student teacher's ability to learn how to manage problems.

- Provide opportunities for your student teacher to succeed.
- Recognize positive change and effort.
- Be available for conversation and discussion.
- Be a good listener.

While it is a rare occasion that big problems arise with a student teacher, it is comforting to know that you are not alone. The cooperating teacher does not carry the full weight of decision-making in regard to a difficult situation. Informing the college supervisor and seeking input is vital because he or she may have additional information, another perspective on the situation, established protocol from the college, or have previously handled a similar situation. At times, you may also wish to consult with your principal. Your input will be needed to present the following:

- Current status of the situation
- Facets of concern
- Potential factors to consider
- Possible input from the student teacher
- Ideas for creating the best situation for the student teacher's professional growth

A compassionate and confident resolution to difficult situations evolves as the result of a cooperating teacher creating a positive working environment, being aware of potential problems, addressing issues promptly, and knowing all stakeholders are working together to create a positive outcome for a future teacher's development.

Note to Self:

✓ There are no evaluation surprises when assessment is routine.
✓ Good communication is good due process.
✓ Effective conferencing matches the development level of the ST.
✓ Evaluation develops skill in self-evaluation.
✓ Recommendation wording matters.
✓

✓

Chapter 3

What's Involved in the Evaluation Process?

During student teaching, major formal evaluations involve an analysis of your student teacher's performance for the dual purposes of assessing their growth and determining their readiness to assume the role of an effective teacher. The process involves knowing the college program's criteria and requirements, analyzing the student teacher's performance, and producing a written recommendation.

Evaluation is a complex but necessary part of becoming a teacher, so evaluation of the student teacher is a necessary task for the cooperating teacher. In general, the evaluation of student teachers should:

- Be an implicit and routine part of the student teaching process.
- Be accurate and based on consistent, observable data.
- Focus on those skills and techniques that are essential for good performance as a teacher.
- Identify areas that need improvement, as well as recognize those that are satisfactory.
- Provide guidelines for the next steps in learning about teaching.
- Furnish a prospective employer and the college with an objective description of the student teacher's ability and readiness for teaching.

The college will request formal written reports on the progress of the student teacher; a midterm and a final report are most common. The criteria are provided to you early in the experience so that you can facilitate your student teacher's development in those areas throughout the experience.

Not all student teaching evaluations are alike. Some evaluations are designed to record the mastery of skills, responsibilities, and requirements at the level one would expect *of a student teacher up to the evaluation point.* A second approach is to record the achievement level of the student teacher *in comparison with a beginning teacher.*

You need to know the evaluation philosophy of the college before completing the report. You should acquaint yourself with the criteria, the rating system, and the procedure expected by the institution.

A special note about developing a positive attitude toward evaluation: Informal and formal observations and conferences that occur regularly throughout the experience build rapport between you and your student teacher. Your student teacher will come to appreciate feedback and supportive direction while he or she builds a habit of professional reflection. A continuous routine of assessment also breaks down the complexities of teaching and spreads the attention across the entire student teaching semester. These continuous assessments will lead to midterm and final evaluations that are accurate and contain no surprises.

Midterm Evaluation

The midpoint affords a good first opportunity for a comprehensive look at the student teacher's progress. Your student teacher has been in the school long enough for patterns to emerge but has enough time remaining so that concentrated effort can be devoted to improvement. A comprehensive evaluation, written and discussed, can be reassuring and enlightening to your student teacher both in terms of progress and delineating goals for the remaining experience.

Final Evaluation

The final evaluation will be a report to the college, with a copy discussed with and provided to the student teacher at the conclusion of the experience. This report will reflect criteria of skills, competencies, and disposition which have been considered throughout student teaching experience. The profile indicates both strong points and weak skills and traits.

This evaluative time between you and your student teacher may be the final opportunity to communicate formally on the intricacies of your student teacher's professional growth and to discuss the most conducive type of teaching position based on your student teacher's demonstrated abilities.

EVALUATION METHODS

Although a college supervisor may be the evaluator of record, most college supervisors rely heavily on feedback from the cooperating teacher. Evaluating the merits and quality of another person's work is a demanding task.

There are potential problems that can arise in the evaluation role. The first is that of objectivity. Brucklacher (1998) states that cooperating teachers may rate student teachers too high because they fear that lower evaluations could damage their relationship. Second, consistency needs attention. A cooperating teacher must guard against allowing her own proclivities to lead her away from a set of evaluation criteria or guidelines. Finally, a cooperating teacher must be aware of her own acquired skills and knowledge of evaluative procedures. These include observation and conferencing skills, as well as knowledge of the instruments and techniques used for successful evaluation.

A variety of tools and methods are used for evaluative purposes. The following descriptions present the more common concepts used during student teaching.

Criterion-Referenced Evaluation

The concept of criterion-referenced evaluation is to assess the student teacher's mastery of competencies. The stated criteria help record specific items and actions demonstrating competency for teaching. Table 3.1 demonstrates parts of a student teacher criterion-referenced evaluation that provide examples of specific criteria, their delineated elements, and a record of mastery level.

Table 3.1. Criterion-Referenced Evaluation Excerpts

Classroom Management				
Criteria	Acceptable	Incomplete or Insufficient	Date of Mastery or Completion	Comments
Prepared seating chart				
Learned pupil names				
Shared in daily routine and procedures				
Regulated physical aspects of the room				
Helped with disciplinary problems				
Initiated new management technique				
Contributed to room decor				

Professional Activities				
Criteria	Acceptable	Incomplete or Insufficient	Date of Mastery or Completion	Comments
Attended professional meetings outside school building				
Studied a teacher code of ethics				
Became familiar with professional journals				
Learned about role of teacher associations and unions				

Rating Scales

It is almost certain that a cooperating teacher will be asked to use a rating scale of some type in the evaluation of student teachers. A quality scale will contain a comprehensive set of knowledge indicators, teaching skills, and attitudinal behaviors pertaining to effective teaching. An obvious advantage to the scale and criteria is that they force evaluative consideration of some skills and traits that might otherwise be overlooked or ignored. A sample rating scale with criteria can be found in table 3.2.

Table 3.2.   Teacher Evaluation Rating Scale Excerpts

Instructional	*3*	*2*	*1*	*NB*
Designs effective lessons				
Links objectives to standards				
Has command of lesson content				
Prepares materials				
Uses effective instructional strategies and activities				
Motivates and engages learners				
Addresses needs of diverse learners				
Uses appropriate levels of questions				
Monitors student performance				
Provides feedback				
Uses voice and body language to engage learners				

Professional Attributes	*3*	*2*	*1*	*NB*
Appearance and grooming				
Written communication				
Oral communication				
Initiative				
Responsibility				
Empathy				
Confidence				
Promptness				
Energy				
Collaboration				
Interactions with pupils				
Interactions with adults				
Response to suggestions				
Self-evaluation				

3 = Meets Expectations for Beginning Teacher Level; 2 = Developing; 1 = Minimal Competency;
NB = No Basis for Judgment

Pupil Evaluation

While not a stand-alone method, pupil evaluations offer a different perspective on the effectiveness of a student teacher's performance. Learners
may be able to make suggestions or give praise to the student teacher that
the cooperating teacher cannot convey or does not realize exists.

Your student teacher may have reservations about pupil evaluations if
he suspects that the pupils will submit harsh or unfair criticisms. Some
student teachers will be looking only for praise and can become quite con-
cerned if there is even one poor evaluation. As Myers (2008) notes, there
is need for caution in interpreting the results when soliciting this type of
evaluation. Your experience can assist your student teacher in analyzing
the results from your pupils.

There are various ways of soliciting pupil evaluations. One of the sim-
plest and most popular methods is a rating scale on the criteria which define effective teaching and teachers. This can be designed by your student
teacher with suggestions and review by you.

However, consider that the most informative and revealing pupil
evaluations may come from open-ended questions, as they let students
express ideas in their own words. These questions are less restrictive and
permit pupils to communicate their prevailing thoughts. Consider questions such as the following:

- What did you like best about the class or the student teacher?
- If the student teacher were to teach the class again, what changes
  could be made that would be more helpful to you?

Self-Evaluation

If a student teacher is to become a responsible teacher, he or she must
be able to evaluate themselves accurately. This ability can be developed
and refined during student teaching. The same evaluation instrument
that you use from the college is a natural tool for this purpose.

You may find your student teacher's perceptions differ from yours; this
should not eliminate the use of self-evaluation. As a healthy and helpful
part of the evaluation process, differences can lead to insightful dialogue
between the two of you as you reconcile the two points of view.

Portfolio Evaluation

One of the most comprehensive tools to document the professional
growth of preservice teachers is the portfolio (Diamantes, 1996). The
portfolio collection documents the ways student teachers meet initial

licensure requirements; the college supervisor will explain the requirements and documentation criteria and process. Through this process, self-assessment skills are learned that will continue to be important to student teachers as lifelong learners (Swetnam, 1997).

Dutt, Kayler, and Tallerico (1999) identify several benefits to using portfolios including increased student teacher reflection, enhanced opportunities to engage in professional dialogue, and the development of a growth-validating mechanism. Johnson (1999) also notes the benefit in learning a documentation process for professional development that many states and school districts require for relicensure purposes.

CONFERENCES APPLYING QUADRANT LEVELS

The cooperating teacher shares the student teacher evaluation with the college supervisor. After conferring on the progress of your student teacher, a conference with the student teacher will take place. Generally, it is up to the representative of the college to conduct the conference with the student teacher to provide this information.

If you are included in the conference along with the college supervisor, if you are the one responsible for the conference, or if you have a follow-up conversation with your student teacher after the college supervisor leaves, consider approaching the conference using strategies presented earlier in this series.

As explained in the second book of this series, identifying the developmental degree of your student teacher's abstraction and commitment levels will help you choose the most effective method of communication to use during a conference (Glickman 1981; Glickman 1995; Henry,1995). Cooperating teachers can use four conferencing approaches that correspond with four different levels of student teachers. The following guidelines explain those approaches for the cooperating teacher to follow with each level of student teacher.

Quadrant 1 Student Teacher (Low Abstraction, Low Commitment)

The Quadrant 1 student teacher is likely not at the self-sufficient beginning teacher level, and certification may be questionable. If your student teacher falls into this quadrant, you will use a directive approach. Begin by indicating what was successful according to the criteria on the evaluation report. Follow with a listing of first-year teaching expectations and a plan for additional ways to obtain necessary skills and experiences prior to the outset of a teaching career. If this is a midterm conference, then the focus will be on defining a plan for the second half of student teaching.

Quadrant 2 Student Teacher (Low Abstraction, High Commitment)

If your student teacher is categorized in Quadrant 2, your conference approach will define strengths and weaknesses but should then ask for analysis and action by your student teacher. A cooperating teacher might say, "We rate you as needing more clarity in your directions and needing to expand your knowledge of students with special needs. Let's discuss ways to increase your success and let you decide what to tackle before your first teaching position, or during the next half of your student teaching experience." This is still a directive approach, but it lets the student teacher make decisions after options are presented.

Quadrant 3 Student Teacher (High Abstraction, Low Commitment)

The Quadrant 3 student teacher responds to a collegial conferencing approach during evaluation. Both parties offer a critique and determine a plan of action. For example, the two of you may discuss what each person feels are strengths and weaknesses. Determine concrete ideas for improvement and the benefits to instructor and learners. Finally, set a specific schedule for action.

Quadrant 4 Student Teacher (High Abstraction, High Commitment)

For a student teacher at this level, the cooperating teacher uses an indirect approach to the conference. You provide your evaluation report, but only after the student teacher has ample time to self-evaluate. It is not necessary to review the report in detail. Your student teacher's comments may lead the conference topics, and if your student teacher's self-analysis omits a major point, then a gentle prodding question should get the student teacher to verbalize a path to address the concern.

LETTER OF RECOMMENDATION

Before your student teacher's experience ends, he may ask you to write a letter of recommendation to use as he pursues his first teaching job. This important letter places the evaluation of the student teacher into a narrative format. Choosing the right words to describe the competency level of your student teacher is an important responsibility.

What type of teaching professional has the student teacher evolved into? What have they demonstrated consistently? Finding concise and fair words to truthfully and accurately portray the teacher candidate is a writing task, no matter the achievement level of the student teacher. Construction tips for the letter of recommendation follow.

Letters recommending student teachers are concise and informative. Most will be one page long. They begin with a heading if not on letterhead stationery, and they will open with a generic greeting, since the letter will likely be used in several searches.

Here is a checklist of topic areas to include in the body of the letter. All categories are key points of information for school administrators in determining if their school setting would be a good fit for your student teacher:

- ☐ *Introduction*: Grade level and length of time of the student teaching placement, a brief description of the pupils and school setting, the number of times you have acted as both a teacher and a cooperating teacher
- ☐ *Instructional competencies*: Planning, presentation, instructional techniques, communication, technology skills, assessment, etc.
- ☐ *Non-instructional competencies*: Classroom management, after-school programs, volunteer activities, conferences, grading, etc.
- ☐ *Disposition and personality*: Interactions with students, parents, and staff, overall attitude, maturity level, work ethic, attendance, etc.
- ☐ *Recommendation statement*: A final statement of your belief in the ability of the student teacher

It is not necessary, nor is it advisable, to address all of the factors in each category above. In order to highlight your student teacher's uniqueness, choose one or two factors from each of the middle three categories and expand upon them through a vivid example of your student teacher's actions. Your wording can be very influential in capturing the attention of the reader. For example, simply stating that "Ms. Henber has great skills in technology and is creative in lesson planning" is not as powerful as stating: "In her unit on ecology, Ms. Henber incorporated a variety of group activities, two guest speakers, and a clever puppet show to engage her learners. She also designed a highly successful website to reinforce the information at three levels of cognitive development."

While it is much easier to write a letter for someone with high ability levels, additional time for choosing words will be spent on students with lesser degrees of abilities. In the case of a marginal student teacher, the letter from the cooperating teacher may be less of a recommendation and more of a descriptive statement of the student teacher's involvement.

Wording for weaker student teachers may include indicators about the "developing," "growing," or "early stage" skills of the student teacher. Mentioning plans for growth and experience is also suitable. If the letter is written well, the student teacher will not take offense, but hiring authorities will note your concern and can determine if the skill level of the potential employee will be a problem in their school setting.

Additionally, omission of a major element is a strategy to indicate a lack of achievement. For example, if the letter does not mention anything about classroom management except that that the student teacher followed what was already established, it will alert the reader to deficiencies. If the body of the letter is filled with descriptions about the types of learners and only co-planning and co-teaching experiences, this will lead the principal to question the student teacher's ability to plan and teach independently.

In the body of the letter, the amount and detail of support for a student teacher will vary depending upon the professional strength exhibited by the student teacher. You must be accurate, not generous or predictive, in choosing your words. You are providing a professional account of the outcome of the student teaching experience. It will be read carefully by the administrator and/or committee at the hiring school.

After the main body of the letter, end with a closing statement:

> "Mr. Holsp is by far the strongest student teacher that I ever supervised, and I highly recommend him for any secondary math or science position."

> "I recommend Miss Macry for a K–6 teaching position, and I believe she will be an asset to your school community."

> "This growing teacher, Mrs. Gero, has demonstrated adequate skills as a student teacher, and I recommend her for a primary level teaching position or a teacher aide position."

Finally, add a closing and signature. Beneath your signature, include your contact information. This may already be listed in the letterhead but can also be repeated under your signature. It is very helpful if you include your personal phone number in case your school is not in session during the hiring process. There is no need to list your contact information in the body of the letter.

Once your letter is drafted, you are highly encouraged to get insight from another professional. The college supervisor and the principal are excellent sources for feedback and for brainstorming wording for difficult or sensitive issues. Regardless of whether your student teacher is strong, average, or weak, it is normal to tweak this letter several times.

Because the narrative is scrutinized by hiring authorities, care should be taken to present a polished product in appearance as well as wording. The final typed copy of the recommendation goes on school letterhead stationery, although occasionally the college provides an evaluation form that includes an area for your written commentary.

Evaluating your student teacher is the last piece of your supervisory role as a cooperating teacher. Being aware of legal issues and what to do if a significant problem develops, undertaking the written and oral evaluation process, and polishing the letter of recommendation all add to the rewarding role of a cooperating teacher. As a cooperating teacher, your conscientious attention to these elements of evaluation is important to the student teacher, the teaching profession, and the students they serve.

Epilogue

Once the final phase of student teaching ends, it is not surprising that many student teachers and cooperating teachers continue their professional relationship further into their careers. Many student teachers excitedly call their former cooperating teacher when they secure their first teaching job, contact them seeking instructional and management advice during their early career, and eventually mellow into a friendship by swapping professional and personal stories. Whether the relationship lasts forever or just a few months beyond the student teaching experience, cooperating teachers find success and affect teacher education in a lasting way when they supervise student teachers in a purposeful, professional way.

The purpose of this book and this series is to illustrate options and techniques to prepare the next generation of educators. As a facilitator, the cooperating teacher must consider all significant factors and alternatives in order to determine an appropriate course of action. The more that is known about the field, and the broader the supervisory skill set, the better the possibility of making sound judgments.

Alongside the college program and the student teacher, the cooperating teacher is an essential contributor to the totality of the student teaching experience. Cooperating teachers facilitate growth, provide experiences, and kindle passion. With support and opportunity, student teachers evolve into reflective practitioners who can comfortably make wise decisions when teaching our children and contributing to the field of education. This does not happen by chance or magic, it happens at the hands of the cooperating teacher; that defines the role as instrumental and should not to be taken lightly!

If you haven't had the opportunity to read the other books in *Student Teaching: The Cooperating Teacher Series,* we encourage you to do so.

Preparing for a Student Teacher (Book 1)
Coaching a Student Teacher (Book 2)

Hosting a student teacher is a powerful way to influence the next generation of educators and impact future learners. It is a role to be undertaken with clarity and confidence. We are pleased that you have taken the time with us to broaden your understanding of the role and expand your supervisory skills. We wish you well on the rest of your cooperating teacher journey!

Ann and Marvin

What Would You Do? You can practice your supervisory skill using real-life situations. Access Book 3 student teaching case studies at https://rowman.com/WebDocs/online_case_studies_Bk3.pdf.

References

Association of American Educators (AAE). Code of ethics for educators. Retrieved April 12, 2016, from http://www.aaeteachers.org/index.php/about-us/aae-code-of-ethics.

Aubuchon v. Olsen, 467 F. Supp. 568 (1979).

Brucklacher, B. (1998). Cooperating teachers' evaluations of student teachers: All "A's"? *Journal of Instructional Psychology* 25 (1): 67–72.

Clement, M. (1999). Reducing the stress of student teaching. *Contemporary Education* 70 (4): 20–26.

Diamantes, T. (1996). *Using portfolios to assess student teacher progress.* Retrieved from ERIC database. (ED405360)

Doebler, L. K., and T. G. Roberson (1987). A study of common problems experienced by secondary student teachers. *Education* 107 (3): 234–243.

Dutt, K., M. Kayler, and M. Tallerico (1999). Assessing student teachers: The promise of developmental portfolios. *The Teacher Educator* 32 (4): 201–215.

Eckes, S. E. (2008). Significant legal issues for inclusion in preservice teacher preparation. *Action in Teacher Education* 30 (2): 25–34.

Ediger, M. (1987). *Evaluating student teaching performance.* Retrieved from ERIC database. (ED282927)

Family Education Rights Protection Act, 20 U.S.C. § 1232g; 34 CFR Part 99. (1974).

Freeman, N. K. (2000). Professional ethics: A cornerstone of teachers' pre-service curriculum. *Action in Teacher Education* 22 (3): 12–18.

Gajda, R. (2008). States' expectations for teachers' knowledge about school law. *Action in Teacher Education* 30 (2): 15–24.

Glickman, C. D. (1995). *Supervision of Instruction: A Developmental Approach.* Newton, MA: Allyn & Bacon.

Glickman, C. D. (1981). *Developmental Supervision: Alternative Practices for Helping Teachers Improve Instruction.* Alexandria, VA: Association for Supervision and Curriculum Development.

Hall, G. (1990). *Legal relationship of student teachers to public institutions of higher education and public schools.* Indiana University, Bloomington. Retrieved October 8, 2009, from ProQuest database.

Harwood, A. M., L. Collins, and M. Sudzina (2000). *Learning from student teacher failure: Implications for program design.* Retrieved from ERIC database. (ED442777)

Henry, M. A. (1995). Supervising student teachers: A new paradigm. In *Making the Difference for Teachers: The Field Experience in Actual Practice.* G. A. Slick, ed. Thousand Oaks, CA: Corwin Press.

Henry, M. A., and A. Weber (2016). *Coaching a Student Teacher.* Lanham, MD: Rowman & Littlefield.

Henry, M. A., and A. Weber (2016). *Preparing for a Student Teacher.* Lanham, MD: Rowman & Littlefield.

Henry, M. A., and A. Weber (2010). *Supervising Student Teachers: The Professional Way.* 7th ed. Lanham, MD: Rowman & Littlefield.

Johnson, J. (1999). Professional teaching portfolio: A catalyst for rethinking teacher education. *Action in Teacher Education* 21 (1): 37–49.

Karanxha, Z., and P. A. Zirkel (2008). The case law on student teachers' rights. *Action in Teacher Education* 30 (2): 46–58.

Kher, N., L. Lacina-Gifford, and S. Yandell (2000). *Preservice teachers' knowledge of effective classroom management strategies: Defiant behavior.* Retrieved from ERIC database. (ED444941)

Monts, D. R. (1998). *Student teachers and legal issues.* Retrieved from ERIC database. (ED428039)

Morris, J. E., and G. Morris (1980). Stress in student teaching. *Action in Teacher Education* 2 (4): 57–61.

Murray-Harvey, R., P. T. Slee, M. J. Lawson, H. Silins, G. Banfield, and A. Russel (2000). The concerns and coping strategies of teacher education students. *European Journal of Teacher Education* 23 (1): 19–35.

Myers, Sandra. (2008). *Student Evaluation of Teachers.* Retrieved July 30, 2009 from Research Starters Education. (AN 31962660)

National Education Association (2016). Code of ethics of the education profession. *NEA Handbook 2015–2016.* Retrieved April 8, 2016, from http://www.nea.org/home/30422.htm.

Reed, D. (1989). Student teacher problems with classroom discipline: Implications for program development. *Action in Teacher Education* 11 (3): 59–64.

Schimmel D., and M. Militello (2007). Legal literacy for teachers: A neglected responsibility. *Harvard Educational Review* 77 (3): 257–284.

Simpson, C. (2002) Copyright 101. *Educational Leadership* 59 (4): 36–41.

Swetnam, L. (1997). *Teacher candidate portfolios: A continuum of assessment for professional development and institutional accountability.* Retrieved from ERIC database. (ED405338)

Wagner, P. H. (2008). The legal preparedness of preservice teachers. *Action in Teacher Education* 30 (2): 4–14.

Whitfield, P. T. (1995). Assimilating the culture of teaching: The student teaching experience. In *Making the Difference for Teachers: The Field Experience in Actual Practice.* G. A. Slick, ed. 32–41. Thousand Oaks, CA: Corwin Press.

About the Authors

Marvin Henry served as professor of education and chairperson of curriculum and instruction at Indiana State University, where he was also a supervisor and field director for student teaching. He is a former president and a distinguished member of the Association of Teacher Educators, as well as a recipient of its Outstanding Program in Teacher Education award.

Ann Weber served as instructional assistant professor in teacher education at Illinois State University. She collaborated with cooperating teachers while supervising hundreds of student teachers and was also the innovator in developing and teaching an online course in the supervision of student teachers.

The authors' experience, research, and passion in teacher education span over fifty-five years! They coauthored *Supervising Student Teachers: The Professional Way*, seventh edition, which is a more extensive treatment of supervisory responsibilities, and its instructor's guide. They continue as speakers, writers, and advocates for the professional development of cooperating teachers. The authors can be reached at SSTTPW@gmail.com.